Apple Trees

by Gail Saunders-Smith

Revised Edition

CAPSTONE PRESS
a capstone imprint

Pebble Books are published by Capstone Press
1710 Roe Crest Drive, North Mankato, Minnesota 56003
www.capstonepub.com

Copyright © 1998, 2016 Capstone Press, a Capstone imprint. All rights reserved.
No part of this publication may be reproduced in whole or in part, or stored in a
retrieval system, or transmitted in any form or by any means, electronic, mechanical,
photocopying, recording, or otherwise, without written permission of the publisher.
For information regarding permission, write to Capstone Press,
1710 Roe Crest Drive, North Mankato, Minnesota 56003.

**Library of Congress Cataloging-in-Publication Data is available on the Library of
Congress website.**

ISBN: 978-1-5157-4232-6 (paperback)
ISBN: 978-1-5157-4349-1 (ebook pdf)

Editorial Credits
Lois Wallentine, editor; Timothy Halldin and James Franklin, designers;
Michelle L. Norstad, photo researcher

Photo Credits
Shutterstock: anjajuli, 1, Bertold Werkmann, 18, Catalin Petolea, 12, dymax, 8, Filip
Fuxa, 16, iava777, 10, images72, 4, LianeM, Cover, Lukiyanova Natalia / frenta, 20,
Verena Matthew, 14, Vladitto, 6

Table of Contents

4

In winter, apple trees have no leaves.

In spring, apple trees have some leaves.

In spring, apple trees have many blossoms.

In summer, apple trees have no blossoms.

In summer, apple trees have some apples.

14

In summer, apple trees have many leaves.

In fall, apple trees have many leaves.

In fall, apple trees have many apples.

In fall, apple trees have ripe apples. The apples are ready to pick.

Words to Know

blossom—a flower on a fruit tree or other plant

fall—the season between summer and winter; the weather becomes cooler.

spring—the season between winter and summer; the weather becomes warmer and plants begin to grow.

summer—the season between spring and fall; the weather is at its warmest.

winter—the season between fall and spring; the weather is at its coldest.

Read More

Burckhardt, Ann L. *Apples.* Mankato, Minn.: Bridgestone Books, 1996.

Davies, Kay and Wendy Oldfield. *My Apple.* First Step Science. Milwaukee: Gareth Stevens Publishing, 1994.

Internet Sites

FactHound offers a safe, fun way to find Internet sites related to this book. All of the sites on FactHound have been researched by our staff.

Here's all you do:

Visit *www.facthound.com*

FactHound will fetch the best sites for you!

Note to Parents and Teachers

This book describes and illustrates apple trees in each season. The text repeats to assist the beginning reader. The concepts of "no," "some," and "many" are introduced. The photographs clearly illustrate the text and support the reader in making meaning from the words. Children may need assistance in using the Table of Contents, Words to Know, Read More, Internet Sites, and Index/Word List sections of the book.

Index/Word List

Word Count: 62
Early-Intervention Level: 5

24